Tuna

A Buddy Book by
Deborah Coldiron

ABDO
Publishing Company

UNDERWATER WORLD

VISIT US AT
www.abdopublishing.com

Published by ABDO Publishing Company, 8000 West 78th Street, Edina, Minnesota 55439.

Copyright © 2009 by Abdo Consulting Group, Inc. International copyrights reserved in all countries. No part of this book may be reproduced in any form without written permission from the publisher. Buddy Books™ is a trademark and logo of ABDO Publishing Company.

Printed in the United States.

Coordinating Series Editor: Sarah Tieck
Contributing Editor: Michael P. Goecke
Graphic Design: Deborah Coldiron
Cover Photograph: SeaPics.com
Interior Photographs/Illustrations: Clipart.com (page 29); iStockphoto.com: Marco Crisari (page 17), Robert Pernell (page 23), Susanna Pershern (page 23), Roberto A. Sanchez (page 28), Dan Schmitt (page 19); Minden Pictures: Norbert Wu (page 7); NATIONALGEOGRAPHICSTOCK.COM: David Doubilet/National Geographic Image Collection (page 18, 21, 27); Peter Arnold: BIOS/Peter Arnold Inc. (page 20), ullstein–Lange/Peter Arnold Inc. (page 17); Photos.com (page 5, 19, 20, 27, 30); SeaPics.com: (page 9, 16), Chris Fallows (page 13), Masa Ushioda (page 17, 25)

Library of Congress Cataloging-in-Publication Data

Coldiron, Deborah.
 Tuna / Deborah Coldiron.
     p. cm.-- (Underwater world)
 Includes index.
 ISBN 978-1-60453-140-4
 1. Tuna--Juvenile literature. I. Title.

QL638.S35C55 2009
597'.783 -- dc22

                                        2008005054

Table Of Contents

The World Of Tuna

Every living creature needs water. Some animals not only need water, they live in it, too.

Scientists have found more than 250,000 kinds of plants and animals living underwater. And, they believe there could be one million more! The tuna is one animal that makes its home in this underwater world.

Water covers 70 percent of Earth's surface.

Tuna are fast fish with silvery bodies. They have forked or crescent-shaped tails that help them swim.

Most tuna live in **temperate** and **tropical** oceans. Some also live in cooler waters.

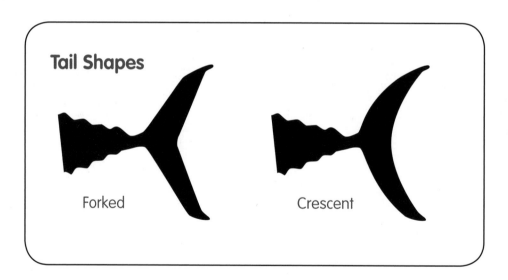

Tail Shapes

Forked

Crescent

Tuna cannot survive in freshwater. They can only live in salty ocean water.

There are seven **species** of tuna in the world. Most have dark backs and pale, silvery bellies. Some have brightly colored fins.

The largest tuna species is the bluefin tuna. It can grow 14 feet (4 m) long. It can weigh 1,800 pounds (800 kg)!

Many tuna travel in groups called schools. Schools are often based on size. For example, small tuna group together.

A Closer Look

Tuna are strong, swift swimmers. Their bodies look like speeding torpedoes in the ocean.

Like most fish, tuna breathe using gills. But, they cannot pump water over their gills. So, they have to keep moving to breathe.

FAST FACTS

Tuna have been observed moving faster than 45 miles (72 km) per hour!

The Body Of A Tuna

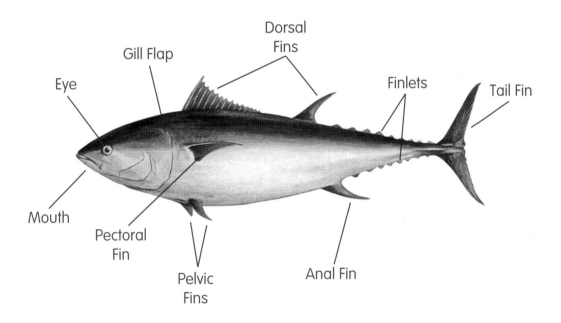

Eye

Gill Flap

Dorsal
Fins

Finlets

Tail Fin

Mouth

Pectoral
Fin

Pelvic
Fins

Anal Fin

Most fish are **cold-blooded**. However, tuna are not. A tuna's body can be 20 degrees Fahrenheit (14°C) warmer than the surrounding water.

Tuna have special **blood vessels** under their skin. These help a tuna raise its body temperature.

Yellowfin tuna are known for their brightly colored fins and finlets. Wild yellowfin tuna live in water where temperatures range from 63 to 88 degrees Fahrenheit (17 to 31°C).

A Growing Tuna

A tuna begins its life as a tiny egg. A female tuna may release several million eggs at one time. Then, a male tuna **fertilizes** them in open water. The fertilized eggs drift off with the ocean currents.

FAST FACTS

Tuna reach adulthood between ages three and five. So, overfishing of young tuna can harm tuna populations.

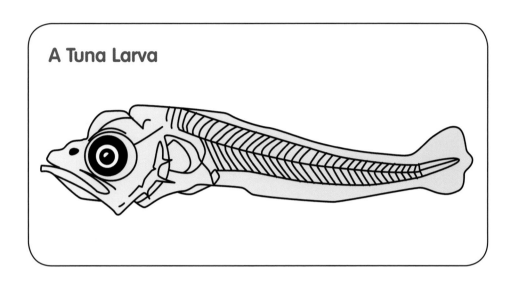

A Tuna Larva

After the eggs hatch, tiny tuna larvae (LAHR-vee) swim and drift near the surface. Finally, the larvae grow large enough to swim in the sea. Then, young tuna form large schools. There may be several different **species** in the same school.

Family Connections

Tuna belong to the Scombridae family. This group includes the seven true tuna **species**. It also includes mackerel and bonitos.

Other relatives in this group share the tuna name. But, they are not true tuna. These include dogtooth tuna, bullet tuna, and slender tuna.

Dogtooth tuna are known as tagi in Pacific nations such as Samoa.

Bonitos resemble tuna. They have striped backs and silver bellies. These fast hunters are found in oceans around the world.

Mackerel sometimes travel in enormous schools. These fish are an important food business. They are also popular with sport fishermen.

Some bonitos are also called skipjack tuna. These fish are caught and dried to make dashi, a Japanese fish broth.

Dinnertime

Tuna are fast predators. These large fish are amazing when chasing prey!

Schools of tuna sometimes attack schools of smaller fish, such as mackerel.

Tuna sometimes feed on zooplankton. Zooplankton are tiny animals that drift in the ocean currents.

Tuna eat many different kinds of small fish. Squid, eels, and **crustaceans** (kruhs-TAY-shuhns) are also part of their diet. Some tuna have even been known to eat smaller tuna.

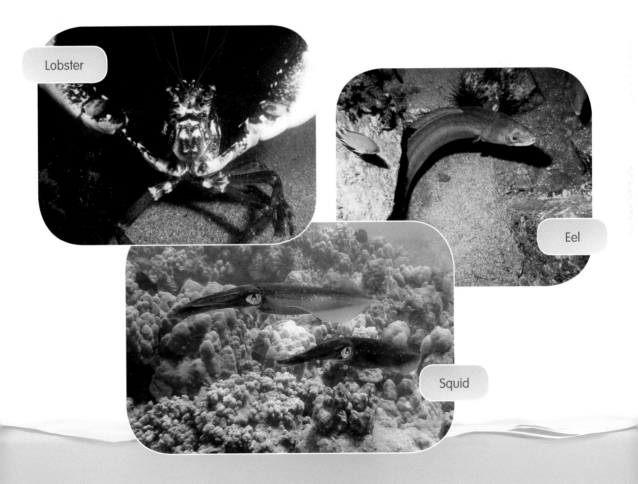

Lobster

Eel

Squid

A World Of Danger

Young tuna have many natural enemies. A variety of sharks, birds, large fish, and whales eat them.

Adult tuna also face dangers. The greatest one is overfishing. This is because tuna is a popular food source.

Pelican

Blacktip shark

Pilot whale

Fishermen use special equipment to help them catch large fish. Some tuna weigh 1,000 pounds (450 kg) or more!

Catching Tuna

Commercial fishermen catch tuna using three methods. These are bait fishing, long-lining, and purse seining.

Bait fishing requires a single hook, line, and bait. Often, live bait is used to draw the tuna to the hook. Bait fishing allows fishermen to catch one fish at a time.

Bait Fishing

FAST FACTS

Tuna is an important food source. Businesses all over the world sell tuna meat.

Tuna are powerful swimmers! So, tuna fishing requires strong poles, lines, and hooks.

In the long-lining method, fishermen use a very long line. Float lines keep it a certain distance below the surface. Many shorter, baited lines hang down from it. This helps catch many tuna at the same time.

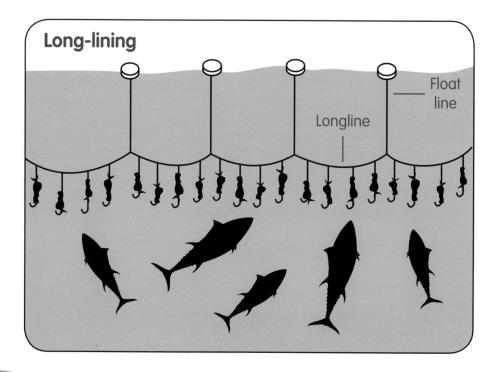

Long-lining

Float line

Longline

FAST FACTS The line used for long-lining can be up to 80 miles (129 km) long!

Fishermen catch bluefin tuna with the long-lining method. This species is sold at fish markets for high prices!

Purse seining involves using a large net to catch tuna. The greatest problem with this method is **bycatch**. For instance, dolphins are often killed after being trapped by tuna nets.

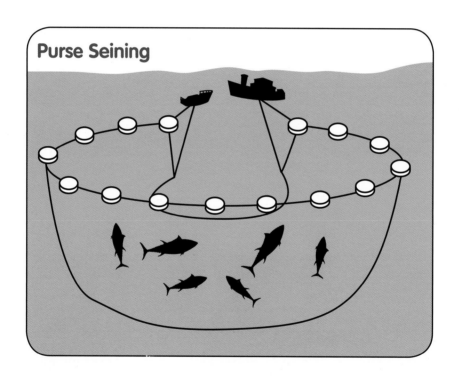

Purse Seining

Sometimes fishermen herd tuna into large nets. There, they feed the tuna so they gain weight. When the tuna are large enough, they are killed and sold.

Dolphins often swim with groups of yellowfin tuna. Scientists do not know why they swim together. But, it leads to a lot of dolphin bycatch.

Fascinating Facts

➤ Bluefin tuna can live between 15 and 30 years!

➤ Tuna meat is a good source of omega-3 fatty acids. These are good for maintaining a healthy heart.

Raw tuna meat is red. But like most meats, it changes color during cooking.

Tuna are among the fastest fish in the ocean. A tuna's strong, **streamlined** body is built for speed. Some scientists have even studied the shape of tuna to **design** vehicles and aircraft!

Tuna is popular among sport fishermen. Many fishermen call it the greatest **trophy** fish!

Bait fishing for tuna has been a hot sport for many years.

Learn And Explore

Tuna is safe to eat. But, scientists say eating tuna too often can be harmful to humans.

Large tuna can have high levels of mercury in their bodies. Mercury is toxic to humans.

Health officials recommend limiting the amount eaten each week. This is especially important for children.

In Japan, raw tuna is a popular meal. Raw bluefin tuna with rice is called toro nigiri.

IMPORTANT WORDS

blood vessel the channel that moves blood through the body.

bycatch unwanted or accidentally caught sea animals.

cold-blooded having a body temperature similar to one's surroundings.

commercial related to business.

crustacean any of a group of animals with hard shells that live mostly in water. Crabs, lobsters, and shrimp are all crustaceans.

design to plan the form and structure of.

fertilize to make fertile. Something that is fertile is capable of growing or developing.

species living things that are very much alike.

streamlined having a shape that reduces the resistance to motion when moving through air or water.

temperate having neither very hot nor very cold weather.

trophy a game animal or fish suitable for mounting.

tropical having warm temperatures.

WEB SITES

To learn more about tuna, visit ABDO Publishing Company on the World Wide Web. Web sites about tuna are featured on our Book Links page. These links are routinely monitored and updated to provide the most current information available.

www.abdopublishing.com

INDEX